CALGARY
& ALBERTA

B. Mitchell

CLB 2130
© 1988 Colour Library Books Ltd., Guildford, Surrey, England
Printed and bound in Barcelona, Spain by Cronion, S.A.
All rights reserved
ISBN 0 86283 521 6

Alberta is probably the most privileged of Canada's provinces, for not only does it possess great scenic beauty but it is also rich in natural resources. The last of the provinces to be settled, the discovery of vast deposits of coal, gas and, most importantly, oil turned Alberta into an energetic pioneer land, suddenly peopled by hard-working settlers and brilliant entrepreneurs, its landscapes providing backdrops to burgeoning towns that have since grown into glittering cities, such as Calgary.

Alberta's oil was first discovered in 1912, in the Turner Valley near Calgary. This field produced nearly ten percent of Canada's oil throughout the 1920s and 30s, then in 1947 the huge Leduc field was found. Within a year this contained 23 producing wells. The giant Pembina field that was subsequently discovered proved to be even more productive and Alberta experienced a boom that accelerated dramatically with the 1973 OPEC oil crisis. Immense reserves have still not been fully exploited, and it is estimated that over 50% of Alberta's oil is still trapped beyond the reach of present technology.

Well over 500 oil and gas exploration and production companies are based in Calgary, giving it the status of the "oil capital" of Alberta and, some claim, of Canada as a whole. However, the city's beginnings concern one of the country's most famous institutions, for it started out in 1875 as a fort of the North West Mounted Police, who became the Royal Canadian Mounted Police, or Mounties. They were formed by the Prime Minister, Sir John A. Macdonald, to combat the rising lawlessness and violence that had gripped the prairies. Not only did this strong, efficient force manage to establish law and order and offer invaluable assistance to the early settlers, one of them, a certain Constable Whitney, was also partly responsible for the province's second great industry after oil, cattle farming. In 1877, he bought a herd from an enterprising American who had driven his cattle over the border. The prairies had long been considered unfit for grazing, but Whitney wanted to find out for himself. His animals did more than survive on this "short grass", they multiplied, and soon scores of herds were being driven north from Montana and Wyoming to thrive in Canada's heartland. In 1883, the arrival of the Canadian Pacific Railway brought to Alberta even more cattle breeders, and also arable farmers. Within no time Calgary had become their trading center and this one-time police station on the confluence of the Bow and Elbow rivers became the largest town in the province. It was to be the fastest-growing in the country. Between 1901 and 1911 the population exploded from 4,400 to 44,000. Calgary, the Dallas of the North, is certainly the place to be for those seeking opportunities and excitement, but it should not be forgotten that this bustling, 20th-century city owes its existence to the treasures of the land, and that Alberta's land is as valuable above ground as it is profitable below.

In the southeastern part of the province are the "Badlands", where some of Canada's most remarkable landscapes contain exciting geological and palaeontological clues to Alberta's pre-history. In Dinosaur Valley eerie rock formations known as hoodoos, which were formed by glacial action millions of years ago, rise out of what was once a swampy marshland where the dinosaurs roamed. The bones of these giant reptiles have been found here in their hundreds and the valley has proved to be the richest source of such fossils in the world.

In western Alberta, two national parks – Jasper and Banff – protect thousands of acres of magnificent Rocky Mountain country. Here there are snow-topped mountains kissing the clouds, endless forests blanketing valleys and climbing slopes, and great, deep basins, gouged by long-gone glaciers, which contain lakes shimmering in unbelievable shades of green and blue. The story of this section of the Rockies begins around 360 million years ago, when a great, shallow body of water covered Alberta. Gradually sediment built up on the sea bed and solidified into layers of hard rock, then great earth movements thrust the layers eastward, causing them to crease and buckle like the folds of a giant accordion. While sediment was collecting at the bottom of the sea, billions of unicellular plants and animals were floating near its surface, and it is thought that it was from these tiny organisms that Alberta's oil and gas was formed. Thus it seems that the same ancestral sea spawned both Alberta's most striking scenic attribute and its fortune, and man has completed the picture by admiring the first and using the second. In Calgary, Albertans have continued to build on the success of the early settlers, creating a major center of commerce and industry. This continues to attract more and more people to the province and thus more discover its real attractions – landscapes of unsurpassed beauty, hinting at the boundless treasures of the earth.

Facing page: the Kananaskis River, a tributary of the Bow River, west of Calgary.

Facing page: (top) Maskinonge Lake, and (bottom) bison in Wood Buffalo National Park. Top: the southern reaches of Maligne Lake by the Samson Narrows, (above) a nodding donkey, and (left) silos near Ponoka.

Right: a field of rape and a farm in Fairview, (bottom right) farmland near Beaverlodge, and (below) yellow poppies. The Alaska Highway (remaining pictures) joins Alaska's Fairbanks to Dawson Creek in British Columbia, passing some of Alberta's finest scenery.

Above: the round platform of the Mount Sulphur gondola terminal and the town of Banff, in the magnificent Canadian Rockies, and (right) nearby Banff Springs Hotel, on the banks of the Bow River. Overleaf: (left) Lake Louise Ski Resort and (right) Cirrus Mountain and Sunwapta Pass.

Top left: a dog-sled team at Lake Louise in Banff National Park, and (remaining pictures) the animals of the Rockies, a fascinating mixture of prairie, forest and arctic creatures.

13

Previous pages: (left) Crowfoot Mountain in
Banff National Park, and (right) the Athabasca
River. Top: hikers on the Columbia Icefield.
Remaining pictures: views of the Rocky
Mountains (above) near Banff, (right)
overlooking Moraine Lake in the Valley of the
Ten Peaks and (facing page bottom) by Peyto
Lake, which appears turquoise due to glacial silt
suspended in it. Overleaf: Lake Louise in winter.

Among the attractions of Banff National Park (these pages) are Mount Rundle (right), which is known as a dipping layered mountain and overlooks Vermilion Lake, Lake Louise (above and top), and the luxurious Château Lake Louise Hotel (facing page top).

Previous pages: the Bow River near Lake Louise, overlooked by Mount Eisenhower (right). Left: Lake Louise encircled by the snow-capped Rockies. Millions of years ago these mountains were horizontal bands of rock beneath a sea bed. On being pushed upwards some of them, such as Mount Rundle (bottom), folded and buckled. Below: Moraine Lake in Banff National Park.

These pages: winter scenes in Banff National Park, one of whose main attractions Lake Louise (above). First called Emerald Lake due to its curious green color, the lake was renamed for Princess Louise, daughter of Queen Victoria and wife of Lord Lorne, the Governor-General of Canada. Overleaf: the thrusting, modern skyline of Calgary.

These pages and overleaf: Calgary, featuring the red and white Calgary Tower (above), Stampede Park (right) and the Glenmore Reservoir (overleaf right).

Previous pages: the grandstand at Stampede Park, backed by the towers of downtown Calgary. One of Canada's fastest-growing cities, Calgary (these pages and overleaf) has developed at an amazing rate since it originated in 1875 as a North West Mounted Police post.

For ten days every July, the thriving, 20th-century city of Calgary steps back into the past with its famous stampede (these pages and overleaf). A spectacular parade, including Mounties (above), ushers in an exciting programme of sporting events hailing from the days of the Wild West.

A popular feature of the Calgary Stampede's parade is the Musical Ride of the Royal Canadian Mounted Police – the Mounties (these pages). Formed in 1873 to bring law and order to the wild North West, the Mounties are today a modern, fast-moving police force. Happily, they still maintain the precision horsemanship of bygone days.

In the days of the Wild West, skills such as cattle wrestling and wild horse riding were essential to a cowboy's way of life. Nowadays, at the Calgary Stampede (these pages), these skills are practised for sport and can win competitors, who come from all over Canada and the United States, thousands of dollars in prize money. Below: some of the horse riding displays require talents that would seem to bear little relevance to life on the range. Overleaf: the dazzling illuminations of downtown Calgary at night.

Literally thousands of spectators and competitors come to the Calgary Stampede (these pages and overleaf), most contributing to the Old West atmosphere by wearing cowboy boots, jeans, hats and checkered shirts. Even more colorful in their traditional dress are the Indians (above and left), who proudly don fantastic feather headdresses and beautifully-patterned costumes. Top: an accident-prone clown brings a touch of comedy to the parade.

Above: the Calgary Tower, with its observation deck and revolving restaurant, dominating the city at night, and (left) the eye-catching sculpture *Family of Man* by Mario Armengol, outside Calgary's Education Centre. Top: Fort Edmonton Park, where restorations and recreated buildings bring to life the history of Edmonton, beginning with its days as a fur trading post. Overleaf: Calgary at dusk.

Dinosaur Provincial Park, with its curious hoodoos (below), is one of the fascinating areas in Alberta where scientists have unearthed the fossilized remains of dinosaurs. Bottom: bison grazing the prairie beneath the mountains of Waterton Lakes National Park, and (right) a view of Upper Waterton Lake from Bear's Hump Ridge. Overleaf: fertile farmland and deeply-eroded river gullies near Drumheller.

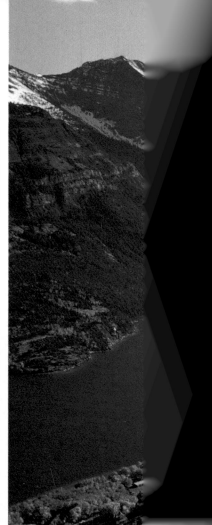

Alberta's "Badlands" comprise some of Canada's most exciting scenery, including the hoodoos in Dinosaur Valley (left and above), Dinosaur Provincial Park (above center), and Writing-on-Stone Provincial Park (top), which contains numerous Indian rock carvings and paintings. Overleaf: a tranquil Albertan lake.